STEP–BY–STEP

Garnishing

How to succeed with garnishes

Wendy Veale

CHARTWELL
BOOKS, INC.

A QUINTET BOOK

ISBN: 0-7858-0340-8

This book was designed and produced by
Quintet Publishing Limited
6, Blundell Street
London N7 9BH

Creative Director: Peter Bridgewater
Designer: Terry Jeavons
Project Editor: Judith Simons
Editors: Sophie Hale, Beverly LeBlanc
Photographer: Ian Howes
Home Economist: Wendy Veale
Jacket Design: Nik Morley

Typeset in Great Britain by
Central Southern Typesetters, Eastbourne
Manufactured in China by
Regent Publishing Services Limited.

This edition produced for sale in the USA,
its territories and dependencies only.

Published by Chartwell Books
A Division of Book Sales, Inc.
P.O. Box 7100
Edison, New Jersey 08818–7100

Contents

INTRODUCTION

The perfect garnish should make a dish look both decorative and appetizing. But not only that; a garnish is an affectionate gesture, a compliment to your guests as well as a complement to the food.

In classical French cookery the title of a dish referred simply to the ingredients of its crowning glory, or a famous city, event or person for whom it was created. (Thus 'Mozart' conjures for the gastronome subtle harmonies of artichoke hearts stuffed with celery purée, soufflé potatoes and pepper sauce.)

Those great dishes live on, but beside them has grown up a whole new concept of garnishing, a renaissance inspired by ideas and ingredients from a vast range of culinary cultures – Japanese to Mexican, from the Americas to the Middle East, Europe to the Orient – each with a tradition of respect, for both the food and its recipient.

With people becoming more interested in all aspects of food and its preparation (an interest focussed in some part of *nouvelle cuisine*), there seems no end to the range and ingenuity of garnishes. But their role remains constant: to make food tempting, colourful, even a work of art.

It is said (and rightly) that a dish should be a feast for the eyes as well as the stomach. Never underestimate the power of the senses as the meal – so lovingly prepared – is brought to the table: all the time spent 'slaving over a hot stove' is rewarded by that sight, that smell, that taste, and, probably, that round of applause.

Let this book show you, step by step, how to turn any dish into a celebration, and any meal into an occasion.

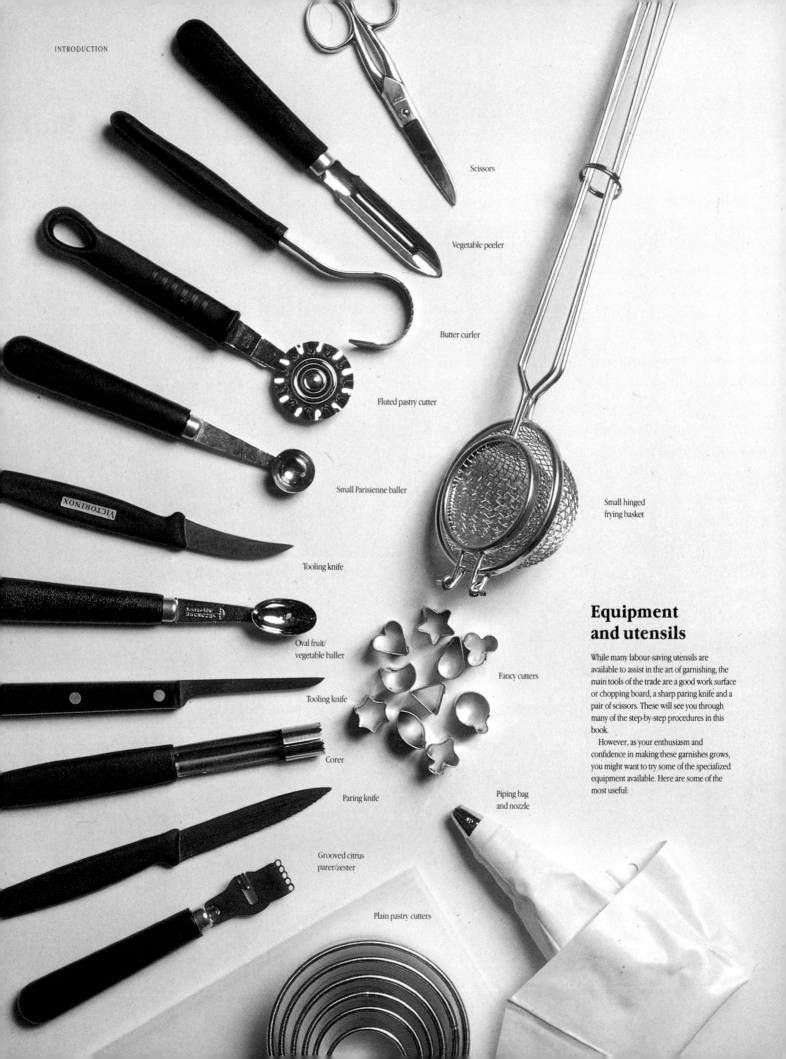

Scissors

Vegetable peeler

Butter curler

Fluted pastry cutter

Small Parisienne baller

Tooling knife

Oval fruit/
vegetable baller

Tooling knife

Corer

Paring knife

Grooved citrus
parer/zester

Small hinged
frying basket

Fancy cutters

Piping bag
and nozzle

Plain pastry cutters

Equipment
and utensils

While many labour-saving utensils are available to assist in the art of garnishing, the main tools of the trade are a good work surface or chopping board, a sharp paring knife and a pair of scissors. These will see you through many of the step-by-step procedures in this book.

However, as your enthusiasm and confidence in making these garnishes grows, you might want to try some of the specialized equipment available. Here are some of the most useful:

Grooved Lemon Slices

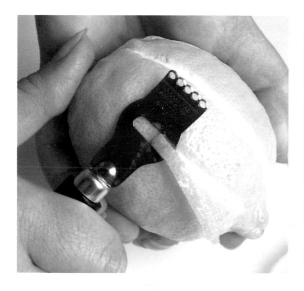

1

Using a sharp paring knife or special citrus grooving knife, make grooves along the length of the fruit from end to end.

3

The lemon slices can be pressed into some finely chopped fresh herbs to coat the flesh.

VARIATION Small oranges or limes can be used instead.

2

Slice the lemon, approximately ¼ in / 5 mm thick, but finer if they are to be twisted.

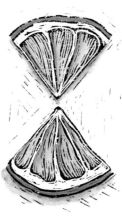

USE AS A GARNISH FOR:

PÂTÉS

MOUSSES

FISH AND SHELLFISH DISHES

VEAL AND CHICKEN DISHES

FLANS

DRINKS AND PUNCHES

Lemon Twist and Cone

**USE AS A
GARNISH FOR:**

SHELLFISH AND
FISH

MOUSSES AND FISH
PÂTÉS

ORANGES AND
LIMES AND
FIRM-SKINNED
CLEMENTINES OR
MANDARINS CAN
ALSO BE USED.

1

Cut a good-sized lemon into ¼ in/5-mm slices, plain or grooved, and slit the slices almost to the centre.

3

For a **Lemon Cone,** form a funnel, slightly overlapping one cut end with the other.

2

For a **Lemon Twist,** twist the two outer surfaces in opposite directions.

A tiny, fresh herb sprig looks attractive in the centre of the twist or cone.

Orange Segments

1

Using a sharp knife, take a slice off the top and base of the fruit to reveal the fruit pulp.

Cutting downwards, just inside the skin, take away the peel and white pith.

2

To remove each segment, cut into the fruit, alongside the membranes of the segment. Twist the knife under and around the other side of the segment, which will then cleanly lift out. Repeat all the way round the fruit.

NOTE Any juice remaining in the fruit's membrane can be squeezed out and added to a sauce or gravy.

VARIATION This method is also applicable to lemons, grapefruits and limes. Try to select fruit without pips.

Orange Jelly Wedges

1

Halve an orange and scoop out the flesh.

In a small bowl, sprinkle 1 tbsp/15 ml/1 tbsp powdered gelatine over 3 tbsp/45 ml/3 tbsp water. Place over a pan of simmering water and heat gently until dissolved.

Meanwhile, gently melt scant 1 cup/200 g/7 oz redcurrant jelly in another saucepan. Stir in the dissolved gelatine.

2

Stand each orange shell in a glass or cup to hold it firm. Pour the jelly into the fruit halves and refrigerate until set.

Cut into wedges for garnishing.

VARIATION Replace the redcurrant jelly with mint jelly and set it in lemon shells. This amount will fill two to three lemons.

ORANGE
SEGMENTS

___

USE AS A GARNISH FOR:

PÂTÉS AND MOUSSES

FISH, POULTRY AND GAME DISHES

SALADS AND COLD MEAT PLATTERS

ORANGE
JELLY WEDGES

___

USE AS A GARNISH FOR:

HOT OR COLD MEATS, GAME AND POULTRY – PARTICULARLY LAMB, DUCK AND TURKEY DISHES

Orange Julienne

USE AS A GARNISH FOR:

SOUPS

SALADS

MEAT, POULTRY AND GAME DISHES

CURRIES AND ORIENTAL DISHES

FLANS

1

Using a vegetable peeler or sharp paring knife, cut the peel thinly from the fruit.

2

Using the point of the knife, scrape away any bitter white pith.

3

Trim the strips into neat lengths and then cut the peel into matchstick-wide strips.

4

Blanch in boiling water for 2–3 minutes, refresh in cold water, then pat dry on absorbent kitchen paper (paper towel).

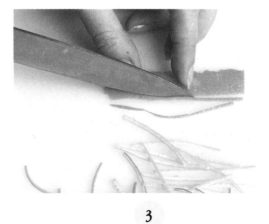

VARIATION Julienne strips can also be made from grapefruit, lemons, limes, or any other firm-skinned citrus fruit.

Apple Peony

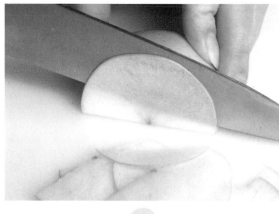

1

Have ready a bowl of well salted water with a little lemon juice added.

Cut an eating apple in half lengthwise. Lay it cut side down. With a sharp knife, cut the apple from stalk to stem in paper thin slices.

2

Drop the slices into the prepared bowl of water. Leave for half an hour. The salt will make the apple pliable, and the lemon juice will prevent discoloration.

3

Take one small apple slice and roll it up to form the centre bud. Place the apple bud, skin side down.

4

Arrange the remaining slices, skin side down and overlapping slightly, around the bud.

5

Use a palette knife or fish slice to turn the apple garnish the right way up and lift it into position.

VARIATION The peony can also be made from white radish (mooli or daikon), orange or lemon slices and tomatoes.

USE AS A GARNISH FOR:

PÂTÉS AND TERRINES

HOT AND COLD PORK DISHES

VEGETABLE AND SALAD DISHES

Kiwi Fans

USE AS A GARNISH FOR:

SALADS, PÂTÉS AND MOUSSES

FISH, CHICKEN AND GAME DISHES

COLD MEAT PLATTERS

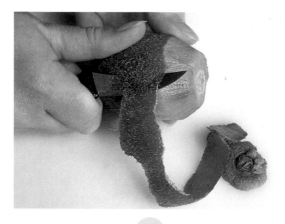

1

Select firm, small kiwi fruits. Using a sharp paring knife, peel off the skin.

2

Cut the kiwi in half, lengthwise, and then again into quarters.

3

Cut five or six slices along the length of the kiwi as shown, stopping just short of the end.

4

With the point of the knife, carefully ease the slices open, and fan them out.

5

A small decorative chive 'bow', or a fresh herb sprig, or a small slice of strawberry can add a final touch.

Melon 'Grapes'

1

Any variety of ripe melon can be used to make this miniature bunch of grapes. Cut the melon in half and scoop out the seeds.

3

Arrange the balls on the serving plate, in a triangular shape, with two small coriander or flat parsley leaves at the top to represent the vine leaves, and a piece of chive stem for the stalk.

2

Using the smallest Parisienne cutter (melon baller), scoop out six balls for each garnish.

4

More melon balls can be built up to form a larger bunch of grapes, 20 to 30, say, to garnish meat, fish and cheese platters.

Poached Pears

USE AS A GARNISH FOR:

PORK, DUCK, GOOSE AND GAME (PARTICULARLY ROAST) DISHES

POACHED FISH DISHES

CHEESE DISHES

1

Select small, firm, but ripe pears. Peel the fruit. Have ready a bowl of water with a little lemon juice added to prevent discoloration.

Cut each pear in half lengthwise and then, with a teaspoon or Parisienne cutter (melon baller), scoop out the core to form a small cavity.

Cut a fine slice off the base of the pear so it will sit upright.

2

Prepare a light sugar syrup by dissolving ½ cup/125 g/4 oz sugar in 1¼ cups/300 ml/½ pt water and 1 tbsp/15 ml/1 tbsp lemon juice over a low heat, then boiling for 2–3 minutes. Add the pears and gently simmer until they have softened slightly. This will take 10–15 minutes, depending upon the ripeness of the fruit.

Drain the fruit on absorbent kitchen paper (paper towel) and either keep warm or allow to cool before using.

3

Fill the cavity with either chopped nuts and dried fruits, or a savoury butter and fresh herbs.

VARIATION Apples can be poached and filled in the same way. They should be peeled first, and a slice cut off top and bottom, leaving approximately two-thirds of the apple. Then, using a small, sharp knife or corer, the core can be scooped out to form a cavity.

Frosted Cranberries

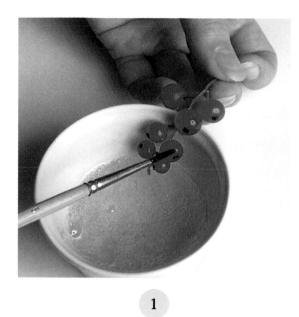

1

Select ripe cranberries, or other red berries, and separate into small bunches. Brush with beaten egg white.

3

Form into small clusters and leave on a wire rack to dry thoroughly.

2

Lightly sprinkle the fruit with caster (superfine) sugar.

4

Arrange the clusters, tucking a couple of small mint leaves in between them.

VARIATION The same method can be applied to black and green grapes, and, if used for decorating a dessert, dredge heavily with the sugar.

USE AS A GARNISH FOR:

TERRINES AND PÂTÉS

COLD MEAT PLATTERS

ROAST TURKEY AND GAME BIRD DISHES

CHEESEBOARDS

Star Fruit (Carambola)

USE AS A GARNISH FOR:

TERRINES AND PÂTÉS

CHICKEN AND PORK DISHES

COLD MEATS

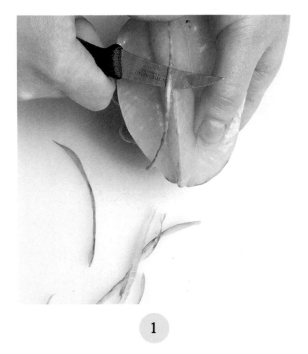

1

The unique shape of this fruit makes it a natural garnish.

Select a fruit which does not have too many blemishes. If necessary, finely pare down the points of the star to remove discoloured or rough skin.

2

Slice the fruit approximately ¼ in / 5 mm thick.

3

Use the sliced star fruit on its own, or with another fruit such as kiwi, or form into a flower using chive stems and herb leaves to make up the picture.

Chiffonade	**Chilli Flowers**

1	1

Thoroughly wash the large, outer leaves of a crisp lettuce, like iceberg or Webbs. Lay the leaves on top of each other and then tightly roll up to form a cigar shape. With a sharp knife, slice the lettuce very finely.

The stalk ends of small red or green chilli peppers are used for this garnish. Cut to the desired length. Slide a small paring knife around the inside of the chilli to loosen the core and seeds and remove them.

CHIFFONADE

USE AS A GARNISH FOR:

CLEAR SOUPS AND CONSOMMÉS

CHIFFONADE IS A CLASSIC GARNISH FOR LIGHT SOUPS

2	2

Place the shredded lettuce in a colander or sieve and pour freshly boiled water over to blanch it. Refresh under cold water.

Using scissors, cut around the length of the chilli to form petals, trimming the tips of each petal to a point.

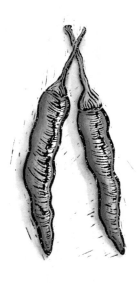

3	3

Sprinkle the lettuce chiffonade over the soup just before serving.

Drop the chilli flowers into iced water and leave for 1–1½ hours to allow the chilli flowers to 'blossom'.

CHILLI FLOWERS

USE AS A GARNISH FOR:

TERRINES, PÂTÉS AND MOUSSES

HOT, SPICY DISHES (MEXICAN AND THAI IN PARTICULAR)

Feathery Cucumber Fans & Fleurs-de-Lys

1

For a **Feathery Cucumber Fan,** cut a 3-in/8-cm piece from a length of cucumber. Cut this in half lengthwise. Then make a lengthwise cut along one of the halves deep enough to remove the seeds.

2

Using a sharp paring knife or grooving tool, cut out V-shaped grooves along the length of the outside of the cucumber.

3

Lay the cucumber on its flat base and, with a sharp knife, diagonally cut a corner off one end of the cucumber. Use the remaining pointed corner as the tip of the fan.

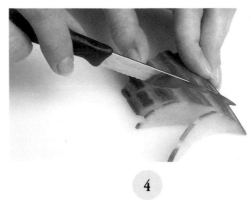

4

Cut five to ten paper-thin slices to the tip of the cucumber (as shown), taking care not to cut right through the tip. On the final slice cut right through to separate the fan from the remaining cucumber.

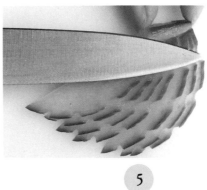

5

Using the flat side of the knife blade, gently press the cucumber slices so that they 'fan' out.

1

A **Cucumber Fleur-de-Lys** is made by following the steps above to make a seven-slice fan. Then, bend the second, fourth and sixth slice towards the joined end of the fan, forming small plumes. Arrange the fleur-de-lys, fold side down.

Radish Bud & Marguerite

1

1

USE AS A
GARNISH FOR:

PÂTÉS AND
TERRINES

SALADS AND COLD
MEAT PLATTERS

To make a **Radish Bud,** select a round, unblemished radish. Wash and cut a fine slice off the stalk end. Turn the radish over. Using a sharp paring knife, make 4 vertical and 6 horizontal cuts, stopping just short of the base of the radish – do not slice right through it.

To make a **Radish Marguerite,** initially prepare a radish as for a bud, then, using a small sharp paring knife, cut 4–6 leaf-shapes, into the red skin only, from the top centre almost down to the stalk end. Ease the red 'petals' away with the knife point, leaving the lower ends attached.

2

2

Drop the radish 'bud' into iced water, where it will take from 30 minutes to an hour to begin to open.

Drop the radish 'marguerite' into iced water where it will take from 30 minutes to an hour to begin to open.

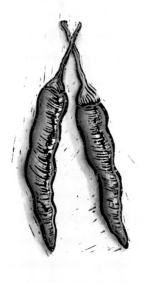

Tomato Crabs

USE AS A GARNISH FOR:

PÂTÉS, MOUSSES AND TERRINES

EGG DISHES

ALMOST ANY COLD MEAT

FISH OR VEGETABLE DISHES

1

Sit a firm, ripe tomato on its stem end. Starting at one side, slice the tomato at approximately ¼-in/5-mm intervals, but do not cut right through to the base.

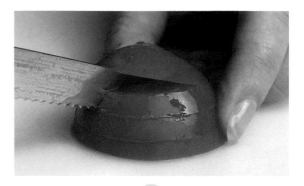

3

Lay the joined tomato slices, skin sides up, on the work surface. Gently lift up the top slice and, with a small knife, cut through the centre of the remaining slices.

2

On the fourth slice, cut right through to separate the joined slices from the other half of the tomato. Using a teaspoon, scoop out the seeds.

4

Using the flat side of a knife blade, gently press the tomato slices out to form a crab. Repeat this procedure with the other side of the tomato to form a second crab.

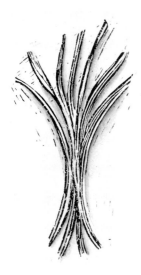

Tomato Rose

1

Select medium-sized, firm, ripe tomatoes. Starting at the non-stalk end of the tomato, slice a continuous paper-thin strip of skin ½ in/1.5 cm wide. Use a small sharp paring knife and cut in a circular fashion around the tomato to produce this 'spiral' with ease.

2

Using the stem end of the strip to form the centre of the rose, carefully wind the tomato peel around itself, skin side out.

3

When completely wound, shape the skin into a rose, making the 'petals' more open around the base of the flower. A couple of bay or mint leaves add a final touch.

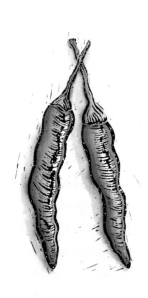

Tomato Tulip

USE AS A GARNISH FOR:

SALADS

COLD MEATS

PÂTÉS AND MOUSSES

ORIENTAL DISHES

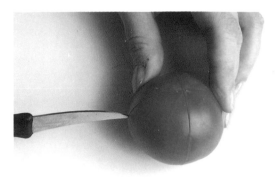

1

Without cutting into the tomato, score the skin into quarters from the top to two-thirds down.

2

Using a paring knife, carefully peel back each 'petal' by cutting between the tomato skin and the flesh to about half the height of the tomato.

3

Gently pierce the top centre of the tomato with a wooden skewer to make a small hole.

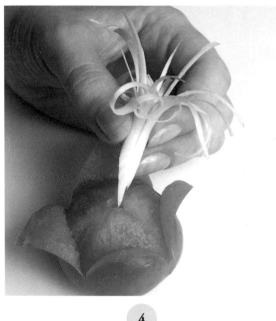

4

Trim a spring onion (scallion) and cut it along the length of the green stem. Drop into a bowl of cold water until the onion has 'curled', then trim white end of the spring onion curl so it will fit into the tomato as shown.

VARIATION A sprig of dill or fennel can be used instead of spring onion.

Onion Rings

1

Select firm, medium-sized red, white or brown onions. Peel off the outer papery skin. Turn the onion on its side and cut slices approximately ¼ in/5 mm thick. Separate the slices.

2

Sprinkle the rings with paprika pepper, turmeric or mild curry powder. Alternatively, toss the rings in finely chopped parsley, so that they are evenly coated.

Onion Chrysanthemum

1

Select a small, firm, white or red onion. Peel away the fine paper skin. Trim away the stem and the root.

Sit the onion firmly on its base and, with a small, sharp knife, make a series of criss-cross incisions, at approximately ¼ in/5 mm intervals. Do not cut right the way through to the root.

2

Let some of the onion pieces fall away (they can be discarded). Gently tease apart the onion to form a tight chrysanthemum flower.

3

Arrange singly, or in a group with a couple of bay leaves.

VARIATION If wished, the edge of the onion can be 'blushed' pink with a little food colouring. Shallots and pickling onions can also be used to make miniature chrysanthemums.

ONION RINGS

USE AS A GARNISH FOR:

TERRINES

MIDDLE EASTERN OR OTHER SPICY DISHES

VEGETABLE AND EGG DISHES

COLD MEAT PLATTERS

SALADS

ONION CHRYSANTHEMUM

USE AS A GARNISH FOR:

TERRINES AND PÂTÉS

COLD MEATS

FLANS

PIES

SALADS

Asparagus Tips with Parma Ham

1

Select tender young fresh asparagus tips, or buy a good quality can of tips. Cut into 2-in/5-cm lengths. Cook the fresh asparagus until *al dente*. Drain and refresh in iced water. Drain thoroughly.

3

Lay the asparagus rolls on their seam and lightly glaze with some aspic jelly or gelatine dissolved in stock or wine.

2

Cut the Parma ham into strips long enough to wrap around one or two asparagus tips twice, and cover two-thirds of the length of asparagus, revealing just the tip.

4

Garnish each roll with a bow made from a small strand of fresh chive or canned pimento, or with tiny hard-boiled egg shapes and red or black caviar or lumpfish roe.

Deep-fried Celery Leaves

1

Select a leafy green head of celery. Discard any tough outer leaves and remove the stalks. Detach small sprigs of leaves and, if necessary, wash and dry them.

3

Drain on absorbent kitchen paper (paper towel) and, with a pair of scissors, snip away the stalks just to below the first leaves.

2

Preheat some oil for deep-fat frying to 375°F/190°C. Drop the sprigs of leaves into the hot oil and fry for 1–2 minutes or until the leaves are golden brown and crisp. (Remove by the stalks as the leaves are brittle.)

4

Sprinkle the leaves lightly with paprika pepper to give a warm red dusting. Long, thin strands of cucumber also make an attractive addition. Use for garnish immediately.

USE AS A GARNISH FOR:

GRILLED (BROILED) MEATS AND FISH

ROAST JOINTS

EGG AND VEGETABLE DISHES

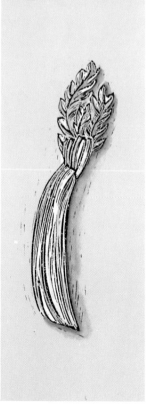

Courgette (Zucchini) Barges

1

Select large-sized green courgettes (zucchini). Split each in half lengthwise, and then cut into 3-in/7-cm lengths. Using a small, sharp paring knife, carve the ends to form a barge shape.

2

Take a fine slice off the underside to give the 'barge' a secure base to sit on. With a small teaspoon or grapefruit knife, hollow out the courgette barge to within ¼ in/5 mm of the edge. Prepare the remaining wedges of courgette in the same way.

3

Prepare some tiny colourful vegetables – carrots, baby sweetcorn slices, baby mushroom slices, petit pois.

Blanch the courgette barges and vegetables in boiling, salted water until *al dente*. Drain and toss in butter if to be presented as a hot garnish.

4

Fill the courgette barges with a cargo of vegetables and some tiny, fresh herb sprigs. The barges can be glazed with aspic if to be served cold.

Turned Mushroom Caps

Potato Allumettes

1

1

Select fresh, white, medium-sized button mushrooms. Wipe them clean with a damp cloth.

Hold the mushroom stem in one hand, and the blade of a sharp paring knife between the first finger and thumb of the other hand. Repeatedly draw the knife down from the centre to the base of the mushroom cap in a curved, sickle fashion. On each groove ensure that each alternate cut is at a flatter angle so that the piece of flesh will cleanly come away.

Allumettes is the French word for 'matches', a perfect description of this potato garnish.

Peel and thinly slice (approx. ⅛ in/3 mm) some firm, waxy potatoes. Trim the stacked slices into an even oblong or square 1½ in/4 cm in length. Slice through the potatoes at ⅛-in/3-mm intervals to produce the matchsticks.

Soak in cold water for at least 30 minutes. Drain and dry thoroughly.

2

2

Trim the stalk and drop each mushroom into a bowl of water with a little lemon juice added to prevent discoloration while you prepare the rest.

Deep fry in hot oil (375°F/190°C) for just a few minutes or until a dark golden colour.

3

3

The drained mushrooms can either be sautéed in butter, or used raw as a garnish.

Drain on absorbent kitchen paper (paper towel), sprinkle with salt and serve immediately.

Potato Baskets & Nests

1

For **Potato Baskets**, peel and very thinly slice some firm, waxy potatoes. A vegetable peeler will produce fine, even slices. For **Potato Nests**, shred the potatoes or cut in fine straws. Soak the potato in cold water for 30 minutes. Drain and dry thoroughly.

Dip a special hinged frying basket into some hot oil to prevent the potatoes from sticking. Remove and line the frying basket with either over-lapping slices of potato or the shredded or straw potatoes.

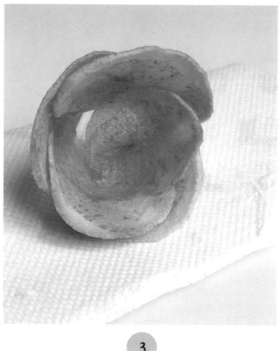

3

Make up the quantity of baskets or nests required and then either reheat them in a hot oven 400°F/200°C/Gas 6 or by carefully refrying as above until a dark golden colour.

2

Deep fry the potato basket or nest in hot oil (350°F/180°C) until a light golden colour. Remove and drain the frying basket. Allow to cool slightly before carefully removing the cooked potato.

4

Serve immediately, filled with baby mushrooms, onions, glazed or puréed vegetables, or Bacon Rolls.

Parisienne Potato Balls

1

4

Sieve some cooked mashed potato. Beat in one egg yolk for each 1 lb/500 g potatoes. Season with salt, pepper and a little freshly grated nutmeg.

Using two forks coat the balls in fine dried breadcrumbs. Alternatively, after coating with the egg, roll the potato balls in flaked almonds or chopped hazelnuts.

2

5

Take a spoonful of the potato mixture and roll it between lightly floured hands to form a smooth round ball the size of a cherry. To ensure even-sized balls, it is a good idea to measure or weigh each spoonful of potato. Repeat the procedure until you have sufficient balls.

Deep-fat fry (350°F/180°C) until golden brown. Drain on absorbent kitchen paper (paper towel). Keep warm until required.

3

Dip each potato ball in beaten egg.

USE AS A GARNISH FOR:

HOT MEAT, GAME, CHICKEN AND FISH DISHES – PARTICULARLY GRILLED (BROILED) AND ROAST CUTS

ALSO AS A VEGETABLE ACCOMPANIMENT

Crispy Bread Cases

**USE AS A
GARNISH FOR:**

ROAST OR BRAISED
MEATS

GAME AND FISH
DISHES

HOT CHEESE AND
EGG DISHES

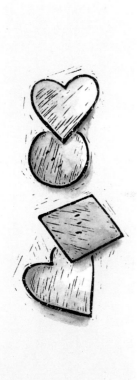

1

Trim the crusts from a slightly stale, large, white tin loaf (one to two-days old). Cut the bread into 2-in/5-cm slices. Score ½ in/1 cm in from the edge all the way round the bread, and to within ½ in/1 cm of the base.

2

Hollow out the centre section, using a sharp knife. Shake out any loose crumbs remaining in the case.

3

Place the cases on a well-buttered baking tray. With a pastry brush, liberally coat the surfaces of the case with melted butter.

Bake in a preheated oven at 325°F/170°C/Gas 3 for about 1 hour, or until crisp and golden.

4

Fill the warm bread case with sautéed mushrooms, baby onions, mixed or puréed vegetables and fresh herbs.

NOTE The bread cases can be deep fried, if preferred.

Golden Breadcrumbs

Cheese Profiteroles

USE AS A GARNISH FOR:

ROAST GAME –
PHEASANT,
PARTRIDGE, WILD
DUCK ETC.

1

Using choux paste pipe out mounds the size of a pea onto a damp baking tray.

1

Use day-old bread to make wholemeal or white breadcrumbs. Either use a blender/liquidizer or food processor for speedy results.

For every 1 cup/50 g/2 oz breadcrumbs use 2 tbsp/25 g/2 tbsp unsalted butter, plus 1 tbsp/15 ml/1 tbsp vegetable oil. Heat the fat in a frying pan until it starts to foam.

2

Sprinkle with some freshly grated Parmesan cheese.

2

When the foaming begins to subside, toss in the breadcrumbs, reduce the heat to low and stir the crumbs continually to cook them to a dark golden colour.

Serve the breadcrumbs warm, in a small dish or sprinkle around your chosen meat.

3

Bake in a preheated oven at 425°F/220°C/Gas 7 for 6–10 minutes, or until golden and crisp.

Immediately before serving, float several profiteroles on each serving of soup.

USE AS A GARNISH FOR:

CONSOMMÉS AND
CLEAR SOUPS

OR AS CANAPÉS

Croûtons & Croûtes

**USE AS A
GARNISH FOR:**

CREAM SOUPS

ALSO SPRINKLED
OVER SALADS

1

Trim away the crusts from thick slices of wholemeal or white bread. (One-day-old bread is more successful than fresh.) Cut the bread into ¼-in/5-mm cubes.

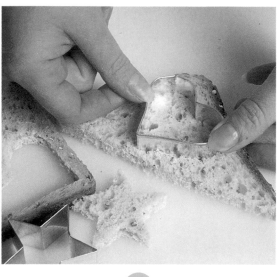

3

Larger heart, round or diamond shaped croûtes can be cooked in exactly the same way and use to garnish meat and chicken casseroles. Use pastry cutters to obtain the desired shape.

VARIATION Frying in flavoured butter, such as garlic, herb or peppered butter can add extra flavour to the croûtons or croûtes.

2

Heat an equal quantity of a good vegetable oil and unsalted butter. When the fat is foaming, toss in the croûtons and stir continuously, ensuring the cubes are evenly browned and cooked.

Drain the croûtons on several layers of absorbent kitchen paper (paper towel) before serving.

Poppadom Baskets

1

2

USE AS A
GARNISH FOR:

HOT SPICY DISHES –
CURRIES
IN PARTICULAR

SALADS

Buy small, round poppadoms – alternatively cut larger ones into smaller circles using scissors. Ideally, they should be 4–5 in/10–13 cm in diameter.

Heat some oil for deep-fat frying. Holding a metal ladle in one hand (or a small metal sieve) and a spoon in the other, hold the poppadom between the two utensils, and slowly lower into the hot oil.

Fry for just a few seconds, during which time the poppadom will curl up around the inner spoon, to form a shallow basket shape. When it is golden and crisp, remove from the hot oil, drain thoroughly and leave to cool on absorbent kitchen paper (paper towel).

Store the cooked poppadoms in an airtight container until required.

3

Fill with finely diced tomatoes, cucumber, sweet peppers or onions, and toasted, flaked or desiccated coconut before serving.

Pastry Fleurons

1

A good stand-by in the freezer are sheets of puff pastry which can be simply transformed into decorative shapes by using small cutters and a sharp knife.

Using a plain scone (biscuit) cutter, cut out crescents as shown. Heart shapes, letters, fish and star shapes can also be made with special cutters.

3

Lay the shapes on a damp baking tray, brush with an egg glaze and bake in a preheated oven at 400°F/200°C/Gas 6 for 7–10 minutes or until well risen, crisp and golden brown.

NOTE Pastry fleurons can be stored in the freezer in a rigid container until required. Thaw out and heat through before serving.

2

Mark and cut out square shapes; cut in half diagonally to form triangles. Using the back of a knife or skewer, mark on a criss-cross pattern. Cut out leaf shapes and mark the veins with back of a knife or skewer.

Choux Pastry Swans

1

Make up a quantity of unsweetened choux paste Fit a small piping bag with a small plain nozzle. Spoon in one-third of the choux paste.

Lightly grease a baking tray, and pipe out a swan's head and neck. This will require a little practice, but is made in two movements: the beak first, and then the head and neck, which is shaped like a figure 'S'. Repeat.

4

Cool the 'swans' before assembling. Split the bodies in half horizontally and then cut the top half of the body in half lengthwise to form two wings.

2

Using a star nozzle fitted in a second piping bag, use the remaining choux paste to form the swans' bodies. Piping in a circular movement, form an oblong, which is slightly higher at one end. Repeat.

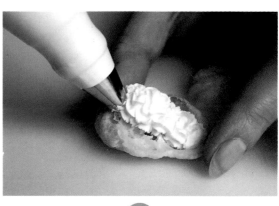

5

Pipe a savoury butter, pâté or cream cheese onto the base of the body. Secure the neck and head in position and then replace the wings.

3

Glaze the pastry with beaten egg and milk and sprinkle the swan bodies with freshly grated Parmesan cheese or poppy or mustard seeds.

Cook at 400°F/200°C/Gas 6 for 15–20 minutes (the heads and necks will need less time), or until well risen and golden brown.

Pastry Horns

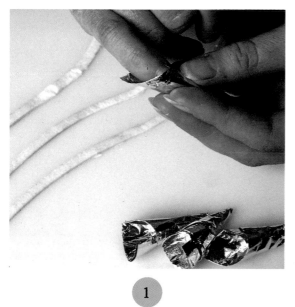

1

Buy a good quality packet of rough puff or flaky pastry or filo pastry leaves. Thaw and refrigerate until required.

Lightly grease either the base end of some cream horn moulds, or homemade aluminium-foil moulds. Stuff them with crumpled foil so that they hold their shape. (The size of the horns will depend upon the dish they will garnish, but they do not want to be too big.)

3

Place the horns on a buttered baking sheet (with the loose end downwards). Glaze with beaten egg and milk. They can be sprinkled with sesame or poppy seeds if wished. Bake in a preheated oven at 425°F/220°C/Gas 7 for 10–15 minutes or until golden brown and crisp.

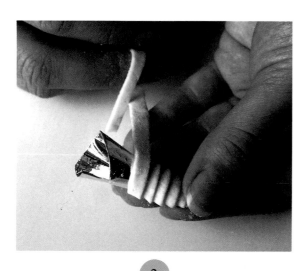

2

Thinly roll out the puff or flaky pastry on a lightly floured board. Trim the edges and cut into strips approximately ¼ in/5 mm wide.

Wind a strip of pastry round the mould in an overlapping coil. Dampen the loose end with a drop of water to secure it down.

4

Slip the horns from their moulds and cool on a wire rack. Fill with smooth pâté, cream cheese or a vegetable purée, using a piping bag, and top with nuts or sliced stuffed olives, spices or herbs.

VARIATION Larger horns can be made and filled for a first course.

Chopped Egg Garnishes

1

Hard-boil one or two eggs, starting them off in cold water and allowing them 10 minutes boiling time. Cool rapidly, then shell and separate the yolk from the white.

Pass the yolk through a metal sieve, pressing with a wooden spoon.

2

Finely chop the egg white and either leave plain or mix with finely chopped fresh parsley.

3

Use fine lines of alternating yellow yolk and the speckled green egg whites.

4

If preferred, the finely chopped parsley can be used as a third colour, with the plain egg yolk and egg white, or the white can be dusted with paprika.

Egg Flowers

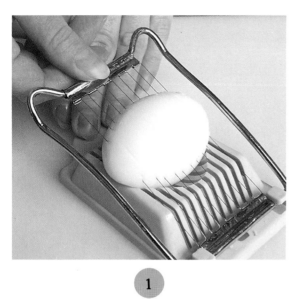

1

Hard boil one or two eggs, then plunge into cold water immediately.

Using a stainless steel knife, slice or halve the egg according to the garnish required. (The egg is most successfully sliced in an egg slicer —as shown—which will produce even, clean cut slices.)

3

Sieved egg yolk can act as the centre of the flower. Alternatively, cut out a round of yolk with a small, plain piping nozzle.

2

The whites can then be cut into fancy shapes using aspic cutters, piping nozzles, and serrated knives.

4

Blanched leek or cucumber peel can be used for bolder stem and leaf shapes. Chive stems and fine herb leaves will produce a more delicate garnish.

USE AS A GARNISH FOR:

TERRINES, PÂTÉS AND MOUSSES

COLD MEATS AND PIES

ASPIC-COATED DISHES

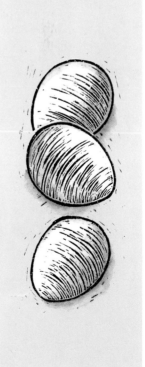

Speciality Butters

1 Máitre d'Hôtel Butter, **2** Tomato Butter, **3** Red Pepper Butter, **4** Mustard Butter, **5** Fresh Herb Butter, **6** Orange Butter, **7** Caper Butter.

As well as presenting butters attractively, as described in the following two garnishes, the butters can also be flavoured before forming into balls or curls or other shapes. Not only will the butter enrich and moisten the food but it will also coat the food with a delicious buttery lemon or herb flavour, for example. Here are a few ideas for flavouring butters before they are shaped or moulded:

● *Caper Butter*
To ½ cup/125 g/4 oz butter, add 1 tsp/5 ml/1 tsp crushed capers. Stir in ½ tsp/2.5 ml/½ tsp each orange and lemon juice and ¼ cup/50 g/2 oz drained finely chopped anchovies. Shape into balls and chill.
  Use to garnish and accompany grilled (broiled) fish.

● *Orange Butter*
To ½ cup/125 g/4 oz butter, blend in 1 tbsp/15 ml/1 tbsp each finely grated orange rind, orange juice and green peppercorns. Spread in a ½ in/1 cm thick layer on foil and chill. Cut into rectangles for serving.
  Use to garnish and accompany fish, pork, chicken and game, and boiled vegetables.

● *Red Pepper Butter*
To ½ cup/125 g/4 oz butter beat in a pinch of ground ginger and a few drops of Tabasco sauce. Mix 3 tbsp/45 ml/3 tbsp finely chopped sweet red pepper. Form into a long roll. Wrap in foil and chill. Unwrap, coat in finely chopped parsley and slice.
  Use to garnish and accompany grilled (broiled) meats, fish, potatoes baked in their skins and vegetable dishes.

● *Mustard Butter*
To ½ cup/125 g/4 oz butter, beat in 1 tbsp/15 ml/1 tbsp mustard, 6 drops Tabasco sauce and a dash of Worcestershire sauce. When light and fluffy, transfer to a piping bag with small plain nozzle and pipe three blobs close together (trefoil shape) onto foil. Repeat. Chill well. Place a tiny herb sprig in the centre of each.
  Use to garnish and accompany grilled (broiled) meats and fish.

● *Tomato Butter*
To ½ cup/125 g/4 oz butter beat in 2 tsp/10 ml/2 tsp tomato purée (paste). Chill, then form into balls.
  Use to garnish and accompany hot meat, fish, vegetable and pasta dishes.

● *Fresh Herb Butter*
To ½ cup/125 g/4 oz butter blend in 1 tbsp/15 ml/1 tbsp freshly chopped mixed fresh herbs (chives, tarragon and parsley for example). Form into a roll. Wrap in foil and chill. Slice the butter.
  Use to garnish and accompany hot meat, fish and vegetable dishes.

● *Maître d'Hôtel Butter*
To ½ cup/225 g/4 oz butter beat in 2 tbsp/30 ml/2 tbsp finely chopped fresh parsley and 1 tsp/5 ml/1 tsp lemon juice. Season with a little salt and freshly ground pepper. Form into an oblong. Wrap in foil and chill before serving.
  Use to garnish and accompany grilled (broiled) steaks, fish and vegetable dishes.

Butter Balls

1

Butter balls can be made by two different methods. The first is to use a Parisienne cutter (melon baller) which has first been dipped in very hot water. Press the cutter into the firm butter and turn it firmly to produce a ball. Drop the ball into iced water until required.

2

Alternately, cut a piece of butter approximately 1 in/2.5 cm square and roll it between two wet butter pats to obtain a round ball. Drop the ball into icy water, as above.

3

The balls can either be served plain, or rolled in finely chopped fresh herbs, paprika, crushed coriander seeds, mixed peppercorns, or finely chopped toasted hazelnuts.

4

If the butter balls are to be used as an accompaniment to bread or biscuits (crackers), arrange the balls into a bunch of grapes. Approximately 30 or 40 balls will be needed to make an impressive bunch. The stem and leaf can be cut out of butter, or cucumber skin.

USE AS A GARNISH FOR:

HOT GRILLED (BROILED) STEAKS AND CHOPS

POTATOES BAKED IN THEIR SKINS

VEGETABLES

Butter Curls

1

To obtain perfect butter curls, a special tool called a butter curler is required. Dip the butter curler in hot water before forming each curl.

Stand a well chilled block of butter on its side and firmly pull the butter curler along the length of butter, from end to end, to form the curl.

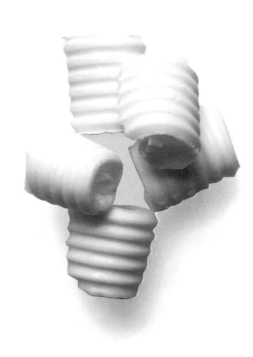

2

Drop the curl into a bowl of iced water until required.

Aspic

Aspic is widely used to garnish foods – whether as a decorative glazed coating, a jellied mould, set and chopped to produce a sparkling border for foods, or used to line serving dishes with a thin glossy glaze.

Traditionally made from strong fish or meat stocks (broths), wine and seasonings, aspic is now available commercially, and can be easily made, following the manufacturer's instructions.

2

● Coarsely chop the set aspic with a knife to form sparkling crystals. Finely chopped herbs can be added to the nearly set jelly to produce an interesting variation.

1

● Set aspic can be cut into a variety of decorative shapes using special cutters.

3

● Coat galantines, pâtés, meat cutlets, savoury mousses and terrines with cool aspic. (This is best done on a wire cooling rack.)

Dip or brush decorative shapes with the aspic and arrange on the tops of mousses and terrines. Spoon a second coating of aspic over the mousse or terrine, if required.

USE AS A GARNISH FOR:

COLD MEAT AND FISH PLATTERS

PÂTÉS, TERRINES AND MOUSSES

EGG DISHES

CANAPÉS

CHAUD-FROIDS AND GALANTINES

Nuts

Nuts – whether chopped, flaked, toasted or fried – offer an abundance of flavour, texture and colour and make an ideal garnish for many dishes.

Always select fresh nuts – once exposed to air, they do tend to lose their flavour and can go rancid quickly. Store in an airtight jar in the fridge, or longer still in the freezer.

● Toasted, flaked almonds make an attractive garnish for rice and curry dishes, giving a contrast in texture and colour. Brown the flaked almonds on a baking tray either in a hot oven or under the grill (broiler).

● Pistachio nuts are a delicate pale green in colour and have a sweet, pleasant flavour. They grow in pairs inside a thin husk, and can be used to garnish meat terrines and pâtés or Mediterranean dishes.

● Walnuts are probably the most commonly used nut in cooking. Whole, halved or finely chopped, they add flavour and are an attractive garnish to many salads, green vegetables and pâtés, and can even be finely chopped in savoury butters for fish.

● Pine nuts are delicious fried in butter and then sprinkled over Italian dishes and sauces, vegetables or salads or into spicy vegetable soups.

● Desiccated or flaked coconut, toasted, is traditionally used to garnish 'sambals', the accompaniments to curries. Sprinkled over a tomato salad, it offers both a flavour contrast and a crunchy texture. It is also delicious on some fish and vegetable dishes.

● Hazelnuts have a very distinct flavour and are most delicious toasted and skinned. Finely chopped, they make a crunchy coating for Parisienne Potato Balls and can be combined with breadcrumbs for use as a coating or sprinkled over vegetables. Flaked hazelnuts can also garnish soups and salads.

● Devilled nuts can be simply made by frying your favourite blanched nut (whole almonds are most successful) in oil and butter until browned, and then tossing them in salt and cayenne or curry powder. They can then be used for Eastern and spicy dishes.

Bacon Rolls

1

2

USE AS A GARNISH FOR:

ROAST CHICKEN
AND TURKEY

SMOKED HADDOCK
DISHES

OMELETTES AND
OTHER EGG DISHES

TOSSED IN GREEN
SALADS

Select some good streaky bacon. Remove any rind and bones with a pair of scissors.

Cut each rasher (slice) of bacon into two or three pieces. With the blade of a sharp knife, held at an angle, stretch the bacon, using firm stroking movements.

Roll up each bacon slice and secure, if necessary, with a wooden cocktail stick. Cook the bacon rolls under a hot grill (broiler), turning frequently to ensure an even colour and crispness. Alternatively, bake in a preheated oven at 400°F/200°C/Gas 6.

Crunchy Bacon Bits

USE AS A GARNISH FOR:

SOUPS

EGG, SMOKED HADDOCK AND POTATO DISHES

MORNAY DISHES

IN GREEN, AVOCADO AND CAULIFLOWER SALADS

1

Select good streaky bacon. Using a pair of scissors, cut away any rind and bones. Snip the bacon into small pieces.

2

Fry the bacon in its own fat in a non-stick pan, stirring frequently to ensure even cooking and colour. When the bacon bits are crunchy, drain on a piece of absorbent kitchen paper (paper towel) before using.

Miniature Kebabs

1

2

USE AS A
GARNISH FOR:

EGG AND CHEESE
DISHES

ROAST AND
GRILLED (BROILED)
MEATS

POULTRY

FISH

SAVOURY PANCAKES
(CRÊPES) AND
OMELETTES

RICE AND PASTA
DISHES

OR SERVE AS AN
APPETIZER

Select a variety of small and colourful food such as bacon rolls, baby sweetcorn (sliced), button mushrooms, prawns, red and yellow peppers, cherry tomatoes, cubes of ham, pineapple and apricots and thin slices of stem ginger.

Cook the vegetables until *al dente*. Refresh in cold water and drain thoroughly. Cut the selected fruits, meats and vegetables into even-sized, attractive pieces.

Thread onto wooden cocktail sticks or short wooden skewers (maximum 4 in/10 cm in length). Brush liberally with melted butter or oil and cook under a preheated grill, turning frequently with tongs, until cooked. The cooking time will vary according to the types of food used.

3

Serve immediately, topped with fresh sprigs of herbs.

NOTE Select the foods that will most enhance and complement your chosen main dish, such as pineapple, sweet peppers and stem ginger for pork, gammon and ham dishes, or bacon rolls, mushrooms and tomatoes for grilled poultry and meat dishes.

Smoked Salmon Cornets

**USE AS A
GARNISH FOR:**

FISH DISHES

SEAFOOD,
AVOCADO OR
CUCUMBER HORS
D'OEUVRES, PÂTÉS
AND MOUSSES

EGG DISHES

OR SERVE ON A
SMALL SQUARE OF
BREAD OR A
CROÛTE (SEE PAGE
58) AS A CANAPÉ.

1

Cut some thin slices of smoked salmon into circles, using a 3½-in/9-cm diameter pastry cutter. Cut each circle into quarters.

2

Roll each quarter into a conical shape. Position three cornets on the plate and pipe a little cream cheese or savoury butter into their centres.

3

Top the piped cream with a little lumpfish roe or caviar and, finally, tuck a sprig or two of fresh dill, fennel or another delicate herb around the base of the cornets.

4

VARIATION The cornets can also be arranged on Grooved Lemon Slices.